WISDOM, AGE AND GRACE

*An Inspirational Guide
to Staying Young at Heart*

FLOYD A. LOTITO, O.F.M.

D0973292

Paulist Press
New York/Mahwah, N.J.

Book design by Nighthawk Design.

Library of Congress Cataloging-in-Publication Data

Lotito, Floyd A., 1940–
    Wisdom, age and grace: an inspirational guide to staying young at
  heart/by Floyd A. Lotito.
      p.   cm.
    ISBN 0-8091-3388-1 (pbk.)
    1. Conduct of life.   2. Christian life—Catholic authors.
  3. Lotito, Floyd A., 1940–.   I. Title.
  BJ1581.2.L6965   1993
  248.4′82—dc20   93-7075
                                                                      CIP

Published by Paulist Press
997 Macarthur Boulevard
Mahwah, New Jersey 07430

Printed and bound in the
United States of America

To my parents,
Filomena and Giuseppe Lotito;
my brother, Michael; and my sisters,
Madeline and Francesca,
who showed me how to love
and whom I love eternally.

CONTENTS

INTRODUCTION

This is a month of reflections—thirty-one short essays in all. You can read one a day or one a week. Take it at your own pace so that you have time to reflect on it, digest it and have it lead you to deeper thoughts and ideas.

You can do it by yourself or with others in a group. There are a couple of questions at the end of each essay to encourage your further reflection and/or discussion.

We suggest this method of reflection. OBSERVE: read the essay and meditate on it so that you understand it fully; JUDGE: apply it to yourself, your life, how to better your life; ACT: do something about it, make a resolution, put it into action.

Theme: Who Are You?

Essays: Appreciating My Unique Self

My Blindspots

Maturity and Myself

Appreciating My Unique Self

We all try to march to the beat of a drummer. We listen attentively for the beat he plays for us. The beat I hear may be different from the one my neighbor hears. So I march along according to what I hear and my neighbor according to what she or he hears. Since we hear different beats, we are on different marches. That's life.

We try to be tolerant. We realize that there are many life styles, many methods and ways to accomplish the same task, many approaches, many personalities, many patterns, many different tunes the drummer plays.

I certainly can't claim that the beat I hear is the best of all possible beats, or that my view of life is the best view, or that the way I do things is the only right way. What is best for me is not necessarily best for my neighbor. I have to be tolerant of others, their outlooks, their ways. There are many legitimate methods and patterns leading to the same result.

A leader once said that we have to blend two virtues within

us. When it comes to principles, we have to be intransigent. We must not give in. We must not water down or compromise. But when it comes to the application of these principles, we must have flexibility, taking into consideration the times and circumstances, the needs of persons and their uniqueness.

The Great Drummer calls some of us to an heroic beat, most of us to something simpler. But we have to bear in mind that it is the same Drummer, although the tune sounds different to each of us. We try to listen, to follow through, to be tolerant of our neighbor who is hearing a beat different from ours. Let the other be. A friend is someone who leaves us with all our freedom intact.

When we all march according to the beat that the Great Drummer is playing for each of us, then we have that perfect parade, that harmonious blend of precision and variety, individuality and pluralism. Haven't we always said "Variety is the spice of life" and "Everybody loves a parade"?

Reflection Questions

Do I listen to my inner self, the "beat" in my life?

Do I accept and like myself? Do I appreciate the difference in others?

My Blindspots

When my brother was teaching me to drive, he warned me to watch out for my blindspots. He told me to keep moving my eyes and even my head, looking forward and backward, out the sides and at the mirrors.

Then in college, my psychology professor cautioned us to realize that we each have selective perceptivity, our own set of mental blindspots. We perceive the world around us from our own unique viewpoint. We filter out what we don't want and seem to pick up and retain only what we want and agree with. As human beings, we all have this. There's nothing we can do about it, but we should be aware of it.

Sometimes we can figure out our blindspots by the nicknames people give us, even behind our back, or by what they tell us when they are really mad at us.

Some people look at Niagara Falls and see a magnificent expression of God's creation. Others look and think, "What a lot of water!"

Finding fault in our neighbor is easy for anyone. We see that speck in another's eye so easily, yet we don't recognize the plank in our own eye. Most religions and religious leaders admonish us not to judge others so that we won't be judged.

The Indian prayer pleads: "Great Spirit, grant that I may not criticize my neighbor until I have walked a mile in his moccasins."

That could be a solution to our problem. How many of us have ever been able to enter into the head of our brother or sister? Who so thoroughly explores others' minds as to be certain what makes them tick, to understand their backgrounds and problems, to know what they have to put up with, their attitudes, their blindspots?

I think that if we did walk in others' "moccasins" for a mile rather than hastily judge or criticize them, we would pat them on the back and say, "You're doing a better job than I could do."

Reflection Questions

Do I know more about myself than I did ten years ago? Do I know what are my strong points and my weak points?

Do I judge others hastily or do I dialogue with them?

Maturity and Myself

Two words much used today to describe people and their minds are "open" and "closed." An open person—regardless of age—is alive, vibrant, growing. A closed person—again regardless of age—is stagnant, shut off from all but the few sharing identical opinions, isolated in a world of his or her own making with the tag "Do Not Disturb!"

Again, I emphasize that "open" and "closed" are not bound to calendar years. The excited adolescent screaming "We hate everything old," while wide open as to mouth, is mentally tight shut, a locked vault. Fortunately maturity will pry open that stubborn little mind.

I know people in their thirties living in cramped compartments, shut, locked, sealed and bolted. I know others in their seventies, eagerly growing in learning and wisdom, an inspiration to all in adult education classes with them.

Some adapt to change easily and quickly at any age; others just cannot. Some suffer agonies if obliged to listen to any view contrary to their own. Open people are like expert debaters. Mature people can endure frustration, can control anger and settle differences without violence or destruction. Violence-prone individuals and groups are immature; so too are war-hungry nations.

Yes, I believe that openness and maturity are closely connected. It is a sign of mental maturity to be patient, willing to postpone gratification, to pass up immediate pleasures or profit, to be able to drive an automobile without cursing the other drivers on the road, to be able to build up a savings account. The mature can persevere, can sweat out a project or a situation in spite of opposition and setbacks.

The less maturity a mind has, the more smug conceit it possesses. It takes an open, mature person to be humble, to be able to admit "I was wrong," to say "I'm sorry." Mature persons when proven right do not feel compelled to crow "I told you so." Also they can disagree without being disagreeable.

Mature minds are more likely to be unselfish, more responsive to the needs of others. They have the capacity to face unpleasantness and disappointment without becoming bitter. Maturity confers the power to remain calm amidst chaos, which means peace not only for yourself but also for those with whom you live, for all those whose lives touch your own.

Reflection Questions

What upsets me most? Should it? Do I let it?

Do I see the positive creative responses to my problems, disappointments, setbacks and upsets?

Theme: *How To Be Truly Human*

Essays: *We're Losing Honesty*

Sincerity Is a Well-Liked Virtue

We All Want Forgiveness

Gentleness

Courtesy Is a Lost Art

We're Losing Honesty

I'm looking for the honest person.

A while back I had my handwriting analyzed and was told that I am a "compulsive truth teller." That may be a polite way of saying I am blunt, outspoken and straightforward. But I do know that I am restless with anything but the authentic, the sincere, the honest truth, simple, unvarnished, undiluted, unexaggerated.

I have been appalled by the lack of simple honesty I see all around me. It cuts through all strata of society, all colors, all backgrounds, all economic levels. We have seen dishonesty in our highest officials. Certain channels of the media have lied to us in advertising, in reporting. Among the very poor, I have met con artists who would put a professional gangster to shame.

The business world is riddled through with dishonesty on the part of employer, employee and consumer, with high pricing, gouging, cheating, freeloading, stealing, shoplifting.

I am looking for an utterly honest person—over the age of six months—one who can look me straight in the eye and tell me exactly how he or she sees a situation, no modifying of views to influence me, no slanting, no misrepresenting, no distorting, no patronizing, no manipulating.

During election time when we have so many candidates and issues, I wish we had some reporters whose judgment and reports I could trust completely as honest, not contrived, not pre-judged, not "bought" by a higher interest.

We often hear it said, "Everybody has a price. It's just higher for some people. Anyone will sell out when the price is right." I hope that is not true. I hope we do have values that are so completely a part of the very core of our being that those values will not be compromised, sold or watered down.

Would it not be refreshing to meet honesty again in our neighbors, our leaders, our teachers, our white and blue collar workers, our clergy, OURSELVES? Again, "It has to begin with me!" I have to be honest with myself and those with whom I come into contact. Sometimes undiluted truth is like unsweetened medicine to swallow, difficult to take, but once I accept it or speak it, I sleep better through the night. That once popular song says, "I've got to be me." "Being me" means being true to myself and others.

Reflection Questions

We have been described as "people of the lie." Am I able to be honest with some people? All people?

Do I find it easier living with the truth, rather than denying it?

Sincerity Is a Well-Liked Virtue

When in college, I belonged to a choral group. Early one morning—perhaps too early—we tried to sing a tribute to a graduate who had returned to visit us. Our efforts could hardly have gone worse. Afterward, one of our group apologized to the graduate: "Sorry about that. It came from our hearts, but it got stuck in our throats."

How often this happens to us in life! We mean well. We plan well. But when we try to express a thought or to perform an action, the result is not what we intended. Many of us find it difficult to articulate what we are actually feeling, what we wish, what we want to make clear. This is a common human failing. But, fortunately, there is a certain quality that can make up for it.

Sincerity atones for a multitude of blunders. And we possess an ability, an inborn perception, an insight, an intuition, whereby we can tell whether or not a person is sincere.

Some people can talk a good game and say all the right words, but inwardly we sense that their heart is not in what they say. On the other hand, some may blurt out the wrong things, but we know they mean well and we don't mind their mistakes. We get good feelings about them.

External actions do disclose something about the internal feelings of a person. More important is to know the real personality within than what appears on the surface. What kind of a person are you on the inside? What are your values, your priorities? To whom or to what have you given your heart? The answers to those questions tell most about you. Then come some externals that are only secondary—how you look, how you talk, your possessions or lack of them, your status, your prestige, your popularity.

One of the best things that can be said about you is that "your heart is in the right place." That means you are sincere, "for real," without artificiality, affectation, phoniness. You might wonder why the word "sincere" from the Latin *sine cera* —without wax—has such a good meaning. It is a fact of history that when a statue was damaged, someone would cover the blemished part, the imperfection, by putting wax in the chipped area, because there was something to hide. But a sincere person, far from hiding anything, is himself or herself without cover-up, without hypocrisy, without duplicity, sham or pretense. The sincere person is not "putting on a false front."

Sincerity cannot be bought or sold or stolen. It is that integrity which we look for in others and strive for in ourselves. It is the quality that confirms all that is good in our character.

Reflection Questions

Do I appreciate sincerity in myself and others?

Has being sincere won me more friends or lost me friends?

We All Want Forgiveness

We all know about the prodigal son. It's a classic short story. A young man thinks the grass is greener elsewhere. He asks his father for his share of the inheritance, then leaves home. The son squanders the money and ends up in a foreign land taking care of pigs. Then it dawns on him: the pigs are better off than he is. He sees his mistake. He gets up and heads home. His father is waiting to receive him. The father embraces his son, forgives him, celebrates his return. But the other son who stayed home does not join in the celebration. Selfishly, he sulks. He is startled, resentful, self-righteous, judgmental.

Well, I think that like most people I have always identified with the father, merciful, loving, forgiving, and have thought myself like him. But someone has pointed out to me that actually most of us are like the son who stayed home, the "faithful" one. If someone hurts us, as an individual or as a community, we are resentful, vindictive. We want to get even. We really do not forgive. Certainly we don't forget. We resent the "bad guy" getting the breaks or benefits, especially when we don't. We're quick to condemn. We don't give a second chance to one who has hurt us.

When was the last time you were hurt, mistreated, spoken ill of? Was your reaction one of mercy, love, forgiveness? Or of resentment, revenge, insistence on punishment?

To some degree we have all been prodigal sons. When we return home, I'm sure we hope to find a loving father, whatever the "faithful brother" may say. If we think this way, we have to forgive as we would be forgiven. We must forgive our returning prodigal brother or sister. It isn't easy; nothing worthwhile is.

To err is human, to forgive divine.

Reflection Questions

No matter who's at fault, do I go first in saying "I'm sorry" or do I wait for the other to say it?

Do I try to get even with others who hurt me?

Gentleness

When my mother became gravely ill, I held her in my arms and wept openly. Later my mother told me that some relatives thought that was unmanly of me.

That took me by surprise. I hadn't played the "macho game" for a long time. I'm not afraid to express my own feelings, whether they be stereotyped as masculine or feminine.

As a teenager I was careful to make sure I followed the macho in all I said, what I did, what I expressed.

As I grew in maturity, I began to realize my own weaknesses. It was then that I discovered that when people admit their faults, their weaknesses, it makes them so much more lovable. One's vulnerability is such a fragile, human quality.

We all need *love* and *worth*. We need to love one another; we need to be loved by another, to be made to feel worthwhile. People with addictive problems realize the absolute necessity of love and worth.

We have to be in touch with our own feelings, to know them, understand them, accept them, express them.

Last month I ate at a small restaurant because the critic writing for a newspaper described it as a *gentle* place. And that is how I found it—with gentle music, a courteous, friendly, quiet-voiced waitress, peaceful surroundings.

Gentleness is a quality we like to find in all people, whether male or female. And we're grown up enough to let men be gentle.

Other names for gentle can be: humane, tender, cordial, genial, trusting, pleasant, peaceful, kind, calm, approachable, compassionate, even the over-used "nice." And a gentle person is appreciative and appreciated by others.

Isn't this what we mean when we say gentleman or gentlewoman? As the song says, "I love those dear hearts and gentle people."

Reflection Questions

Am I attracted to people who are gentle with me?
Do self-awareness, forgiveness and gentleness go together?

Courtesy Is a Lost Art

Courtesy is an endangered species. I see little of it around. Do you? It's not in fashion.

Clerks in stores used to make you feel that you were important as a present or potential customer. Now some act as if you're disturbing them if you ask for something. The current vogue is to be indifferent. Courtesy is disdained as a relic of a past age, of keeping court, the etiquette of the king's household. To show how modern we are, we just pooh-pooh politeness and act as if we do not care.

Do we still have any of those friendly towns where people greet you with a smile, help you when you need it, and make you feel at home? In the city where I live, people are actually afraid of eye-to-eye contact. They do not want it to be interpreted in some unsavory way.

I believe in expressions like "Thank you!" and "Excuse me!"; in opening doors and helping the needy; in visiting neighbors, relatives, the elderly, the sick; in writing "thank you" notes and letters of encouragement. I try to be thoughtful of others and, departing from a place, to leave things in order behind me. I can never understand or condone vandalism; I strive to respect persons and property and the rights of others.

I want to be a pleasure to be with, not an embarrassment. I believe in good manners at table, in transit, everywhere. I respect leaders and others to whom I am responsible.

To test oneself in regard to courtesy, we might reflect on these questions: "Am I able to give orders graciously? To obey them willingly? Do I listen when another speaks without trying to interrupt? Am I glad to cooperate? To be of service? Do I really want to be friendly and kind and patient with each person I meet?

Far from being a mere anachronism or a burdening weight, courtesy is a positive influence, adding uplift, refreshment, brightness to life.

To the doubter I say, "Try it. You'll like it." And remember, courtesy is contagious. Normally the way you treat others is the way they will treat you.

Reflection Questions

When have I met courtesy recently?

When was I courteous beyond the call of duty?

Theme: How To Live Life Fully

Essays: Make Your Own Music

Life and Love Go Together

Loving Relationships Are the Best

Things in Life

Make Your Own Music

"We certainly have a lot of musicians in this town," a friend tells me about San Francisco. I agree and add, "We all make our own music."

We're all musicians. And yes, we do make our own music. Some play it in joyful tones, others in strident and somber, heavy ones. Some can barely be heard; others you can't stop. Some breeze along lightly; others labor along in studied, complicated melodies.

What kind of music do you make? You really can make any type you want. You determine it—not the circumstances or events of your life. I know a lady who is sick, poor, alone, and without relatives. She sings a most beautiful, uplifting song. She doesn't let the conditions of her life bog her down.

We all know persons whose only music is a confused cacophony, or others whose drums always foretell doom. We never hear a happy lilting tune from them. For some, life is a dirge.

Little children make different music. Some smile a short song; others cry a begging ballad.

John Paul I was pope for thirty-four days and made hopeful, happy music that all fondly remember.

Some lives are symphonies; some are popular hits; some are country, others rock and roll, some nostalgic, others classic or even an opera in themselves. Some you can never forget; some you can't recall; some you never heard.

But remember, the bottom line is: "We all make our own music." Don't blame anyone else, anything else. If you want a fresh, uplifting, peaceful song—make it.

Reflection Questions

Do I believe I can change my own life, or that others, circumstances, problems, determine that?

When I am upset about something, do I realize that I let myself be upset?

Life and Love Go Together

The purpose of life is to love. When we love others we bring life to them; they can grow. And then we grow as human beings. Love gives life and growth to others and to us.

I have seen some of the most fascinating love relationships where two persons through their love for each other have grown so much. Some of these have been most unlikely combinations. Truth is stranger than fiction.

I know a middle-aged lady with severe mental problems who developed a love relationship with a young man, brain-damaged and a recovered drug user. Their relationship brought improvement to both of them. I would see them smiling and helping each other. They returned to their religions. They prayed together. "What an unlikely combination," I kept telling myself. Their sharing of love brought life and growth to each other.

We all have problems. (Welcome to the club, if you've just discovered this.) And I believe that the solutions to all our problems are within us. We have to think, reflect, evaluate, sort out. This means that we have to find the center of quiet within us. For some, this also means finding quiet around them. But this is possible for all. You can find quiet within you despite the noise and confusion around you.

The happy person is both inner-directed and other-directed. If you want to find yourself, you have to give yourself to others. Altruism is the answer to your identity crisis.

We want to be truly alive, totally vitalized, and it is our mission in life to be life-givers, to spark life in others so they can grow too. The energy for this is love. Love and life go together. God is a life-giver. God wants us to be alive, to have the fullness of life. Sin and hatred are negative forces; they kill life.

I know so many people who have touched my life with their love and have helped me grow. Sometimes it wasn't easy; it involved pain and hurt, but through it all was growth because of love. Think about it—life and love.

Reflection Questions

Are there loving relationships in my life that help me grow?
What has brought about the most growth in my life?

Loving Relationships Are the Best Things in Life

Above my desk a small plaque bids me: "Plant a little love and watch your garden grow." I've been thinking about that. How true it is! Other seekers of truth have voiced similar thoughts in words such as: "What you do for love will always be time well spent." "Love isn't love until you give it away." "Love is what makes the world go "round."

The questions each of us constantly ponders are: "What is the meaning of life, my life? Where am I headed? Is that all there is?" Such wonderings stir during moments when we feel very much alone, or simply lonesome, empty, incomplete.

We really can't exist alone. Our very "be-ing" depends on others. Alone, we hunger for that interflow of love—they to us, we to them. And the more love we give, the more our garden grows.

In my life, love relationships are the most important part of all—my family, friends, confreres, people with whom I work, God, my religion, myself.

Love presupposes acceptance. With those who really love me, I don't have to fear any possible rejection. I can reveal my thoughts to them, my true self. I am comfortable with them and they are comfortable with me.

At times, when we look back on our lives, we ask ourselves: "Was it worth it all? What was happening? Am I happy? What have I accomplished? Where am I headed?"

Again the easy measuring stick is LOVE—what I did for love, loving relationships, fulfillment of love.

Others use different yardsticks—success, money, power, fame, influence, property. But all these are emptiness, loneliness, without love, without loving relationships. Our fulfillment can only be with love. The other rewards just don't do it by themselves. You and I know people who have won success, wealth, power, and fame, yet cannot conceal that they feel lonely, empty and unhappy.

Love brings us life and gives life. With loving relationships interflowing, we grow, attain fulfillment and happiness. Our "be-ing" is intermingled and enriched by other "be-ings."

Again we are reminded that love isn't love until we give it away. It is in giving that we receive; the more we give, the more we receive. This means that we must be willing to take risks, to suffer and endure, to change, to be for the other.

Loving relationships are what life is all about.

Reflection Questions

What are the loving relationships in my life?

What has brought me the most happiness in my life?

Theme: Beyond the Here and Now

Essays: Deepening My Faith

My Vision of God

Cures for Loneliness

Death in the Light

Deepening My Faith

Without faith, life is very empty. Faith gives life meaning, provides a plan for living, assures us that there's more to life than what appears on the surface.

When I saw two movies recently, this message was impressed on me. What emptiness! What dissatisfaction! People grasping for happiness and never finding it, giving themselves to every apparent good—drugs, alcohol, pleasure, power, money, prestige—and never having peace of mind, never feeling fulfilled. In fact, just the opposite seems to result: boredom, dissipation, unhappiness, suicide. What's there to live for? As the song asks, "Is that all there is?"

Faith puts muscle into a flabby life, uses hard times as well as good times to build strength. Faith sustains us in crises.

I'm not trying to sell any one faith or a set of beliefs. Each person has to do his or her own searching. Your trust may be in a supreme being, a religious writing, a teacher, a philosophy, a code of ideals, a person, an afterlife.

Sociologists point out that, statistically, people who possess a faith and practice it, church-going people, are happier, have stronger families, commit fewer crimes, and are more admired.

I think that without my faith I'd find life most mysterious, discouraging, often unbearable. My faith pulls me through life, uplifts me, enables me to grow as a person. It helps me to help others, to see a plan for my life, to trust and be at peace, to be consoled in sorrows and strengthened even in my weaknesses.

A very poor family visited me. They owned literally nothing, but were so happy and joyful. They had so much love for one another, for me, for the world, for everyone they met. I had barely begun talking with them when I realized what it was— they had a strong faith. They asked me to pray with them as they do so often. Their faith strengthened me.

Reflection Questions

What do I believe in? What is my faith?

Does faith help me see meaning in my life?

My Vision of God

I'm not an expert on God. Yet I'd like to share my own idea of God with you because I believe it might interest you. To hear others' concepts has always been interesting to me because, listening, we learn so much about that speaker personally.

For convenience, I'll refer to God as "he" although I hope all understand that he should not be imagined as of either or any gender.

Mine is a personal God who loves me intimately, a life-giver without limits even if we place imaginary limits on him during discussions. I find him more tolerant than I am, more tolerant than others are. He does not force us into anything. He invites and calls, but it is up to us to respond.

God is a free being and so are we. To be free means that we have the choice to do or not to do. So the future is up to us as well as to God, and that future is unknown.

We have a tendency to blame God for the consequences of human mistakes. A plane crashes and people are killed. Some call that "an act of God." Competent investigation usually reveals that the cause was a mechanical malfunction or a human mistake, not God.

Since God has given us free will, we may make mistakes. We are free to abuse the privilege of choice because God does not want followers in chains, a clutter of robots. He doesn't want to compel us in our actions. He likes us to step toward him freely —if we want to do so.

My God is continually a springer of surprises, a hurler of challenges. He encourages me to think, to grow, to reach for new horizons, to expand and stretch, to move ever onward. In a way we humans have limitless potential.

My God is everywhere and in the people and events about me. He is the God of history, involved in the world's and mine. Everything round about me, every individual, reflects him to me, tells me something about him. All creation is suffused with God. A work of art or science gives me a glimpse of his beauty or an experience of his providence. An author shares with me his personal vision of truth and reality, and thus tells me more about God. I see and hear God in people and all life about me.

My God knows the human situation. He is always understanding and forgiving. He loves me, forgives me, and offers me eternal life. He is aware of my sinfulness, incompleteness, brokenness. He heaps love upon me and encourages me to heap love on others, to heal them also. At times he works through me to benefit others, and I know he works through others for me. I see God even in my sin. I do not separate him out of any part of my life.

What is your God like? Reflect!

Reflection Questions

Who is my God? What is my God like?

How does God reveal himself to me?

Cures for Loneliness

Loneliness can be the worst of illnesses. Loneliness can inflict pain like a physical ailment. Like a cancer, it can gnaw on your heart. At best it veils the true you under a dark cloud of gloom.

We have probably felt it on occasion. I first encountered it when I went to boarding school. It expressed itself in loss of appetite, emotional anguish, tears. I realized how much I loved my family, my home, my friends, most of the persons and things I had taken for granted.

In middle age, at times, loneliness meant to me "being alone." Although with others, I felt alone, no one close to me, no one understanding what was going on inside of me, my feelings, my heartaches, no one to whom I could communicate what was deepest in me, no one who really loved me completely and would never reject me or withdraw that love. I have suffered through such moments. They have served as a real purgation for me.

Usually we connect loneliness to old age. Elders have told me how lonely they are—no one visits, no one cares, not even family. Some say Sundays and holidays are their worst days. Some elders tell me there is no one to listen to them. Nearing the end of life, some are alone in a strange neighborhood, striving just to survive. How pitiable!

What can we do about loneliness in ourselves, in others? Turn to God. Pray, meditate, reflect, converse, listen. If possible turn to others, help others in some need. Try to keep busy, your time occupied. Share with others your talent, your love, your concern. Learn to be comfortable with yourself—read, make, watch, create, listen, do!

Loneliness is an expression of our finiteness, our incompleteness. We are in need of God. And God can fill the void in us as much as possible in this human situation. He has given us salvation, peace and joy. We also need others. God works through others.

Augustine said, "Our hearts are restless, Lord, until they rest in thee."

Reflection Questions

What do I do when I'm lonely?

What gets me out of my loneliness?

Death in the Light

Death is not extinguishing the light; it is putting out the lamp because the dawn has come.

There is more to life than what we see, hear, touch and smell. Our hearts are restless. We desire peace, happiness, completeness. I don't think a just God could put these yearnings in each of us unless they could be fulfilled. This is one of the reasons why I believe in an afterlife. A friend asked William James if he believed in personal immortality, and he replied: "Never strongly, but more strongly as I grow older." "Why is that?" asked his friend. "Because," said James, "I am only now getting fit to live."

We are becoming more frank in our attitudes about death. We realize that it is a part of living. We all have to go through the experience of dying.

Families talk more openly about death. They want to share with a loved one an approaching death. It is better for people to die at home with those they love rather than isolated and alone in a hospital.

People are more practical about making preparations for their death—making wills, willing their bodies for specific uses, arranging their services, preparing love and thank-you notes for others. All this is much healthier than keeping death in the closet.

A lovely grandmother had a terminal disease. She and the family knew her days were numbered. They decided that her last days should be spent at home with the family. All took care of her. All spoke openly about the coming hour and how they felt. So when death did come, members of the family told of experiencing a real sense of catharsis, renewal, fulfillment and joy. There was no guilt or resentment.

Lately we have heard much about people who have "died" for a while and returned. All seem to have had similar experiences—a feeling of tranquility, peace and security; they were not too anxious to return to this life in the way we know it.

A neighbor told me that he had suffered a heart attack. As the doctor began working on him, he felt that he was sitting peacefully on a slope under a shady tree. He was at rest and so content, and really didn't want to come back when the doctor finally aroused him.

Many people want joyful, simple, funeral services. They do not wish the remaining family to be burdened with the high cost of an elaborate funeral. There are simple and dignified alternatives. Many wish the farewell to be a celebration, not a lamentation or a guilt-ridden dirge.

After all, the deceased is now at peace, no more pain or incompleteness. It is we who remain who suffer loss and separation. We need to be supported, healed, affirmed by our family, friends and the community.

Death is not extinguishing the light; it is putting out the lamp because the dawn has come.

Reflection Questions

What do I believe about death, the afterlife?

What do I experience at funerals (memorials)?

Theme: *How To Cope*

Essays: *How To Cope*

How To Listen

Give Moderation a Try

Suffering Is in Everyone's Life

How To Cope

Some things are part and parcel of almost every minute of our lives, yet we never talk about them. Isn't that curious? Maybe they are too close to our heart. Or can it be that we want to believe that they don't exist—or that they will go away?

In conversation we seem to be comfortable with neutral, harmless subjects, like the weather, sports, television, current events. We do not like to go deeper or to let anyone get too close to us and find out what really makes us tick. For example, to the conventional question "How are you?" the common reply is "Fine," even when one is miserably sick. An explicit reply might only annoy the questioner.

Setbacks, disappointments, hardships, failures, are part of everyday life, but we usually do not include them in our yearly Christmas letter or in our over-the-fence conversations. But I think one thing is for sure: everyone has hardships and failures.

Some people look at the world and want to see Utopia. Some bury their heads in the ground and do not want to see the real problems we all face. We do not have the power to change the normal course of events in nature and in life, but I do believe we can learn to *cope* with them.

There will be problems and failures in every life—we do not deny that. But the important question is: "How do we *handle* such problems?" Do we let them overwhelm us, or do we remain in control by maintaining proper calm and balance? Do we have a realistic view of ourselves, our strong and weak points, knowledge of what we realistically can or cannot do? Are our personal goals realizable? Do we have that correct blend of intransigence when it comes to principles, and flexibility when it comes to applying them? Do we take proper care of ourselves, keeping occupied, and on the other hand getting the needed relaxation every day?

As the prayer says, "God, grant me the serenity to accept the things I cannot change, courage to change the things I can, and the wisdom to know the difference."

Reflection Questions

Do I run my own life or do I let circumstances run my life?

Do I overplay or underplay the problems in my life? Do I see possibilities?

How To Listen

Seventy percent of our waking day is spent in communication. Only nine percent is given to writing, sixteen percent to reading, and—surprisingly—only thirty percent to speaking. On what do we spend most of our time? Listening! We spend forty-five percent of our waking hours listening, and we are so poor at it. We have never been trained how to listen.

Listening means really paying full attention to the person attempting to communicate with you, putting yourself in the other's place, trying to understand, picking up the non-verbal messages as well as those put into words. As humans, we code and decode. A speaker—a sender—transmits several messages simultaneously. We all talk on a system of at least four tracks. To receive a complete message we have to pick up signals, decode, read between the lines.

President John Kennedy was an exceptional listener. They say he would drain you when he listened to you. He wanted to pick up everything you had to say.

Not with words alone do we speak, but with our tone of voice, pitch, resonance, rate, rhythm. Our body speaks too, our eyes, face, arms, hands, movements, breathing, not to mention our personal appearance, clothing, and even our reputation. What we don't say can be as important as what we do say.

A dialogue is not two monologues. A dialogue means an exchange of ideas or opinions. This means that there must be *listening* as well as speaking. So often when one speaks, the other, rather than listening, thinks about what he or she will say. So no real exchange or growth happens, because neither party has listened to the other. Two monologues rather than an authentic dialogue ensue.

Communication includes both conveying our ideas and also being good listeners. It is fundamentally an expression of love. If we feel indifference or don't like someone, we try to ignore that individual; then we really don't care to communicate.

One of the most pressing needs of today is a good listener, patient, perceptive, loving. It takes a lot of time, but what beautiful new worlds are opened up for us when we really listen and discover the uniqueness and preciousness of another human being.

Reflection Questions

Do I really listen to the other person or do I think other thoughts when he or she speaks?

What do I discover in another person when I really listen and do not pre-judge that person?

Give Moderation a Try

The Dendrite Culture is what I call our age. The great norm governing so many of us is to measure a thing by the extent to which it pleases our dendrites, tingles our nerve endings, gives us enjoyment.

We are in an ego cult, a neo-hedonism. Yet the product of all this is neither happiness nor peace of mind. Rather it is dissipation, depression, suicide. So, as our experience keeps telling us, self-gratification as a steady diet just does not work.

A while back I went on a rigid diet, 1,000 calories a day for three months. I stuck to it faithfully. The first time I could break away from it, I had a little potato with my meat and some sherbet for dessert. It was like ambrosia. Food never tasted so good. There were flavors I never before savored or even suspected. Yet I had eaten plenty of potatoes and sherbets.

"Distance lends enchantment," say the sages. "Absence

makes the heart grow fonder." The religious philosopher says: *Virtus est in media*—"Virtue is the middle way," moderation is the answer. Too much of anything tends to sicken a person. Then, far from enjoying it, you are repelled.

We are human beings with intellect and will. We have reason. Therefore our actions should be based on sound reason, not whims, not sheer enjoyment, not some emotional throb, not a mere animal instinct. Our human dignity calls upon us to act in a reasonable way.

Monks and hermits in our human family have told us—and exemplified for us—what self-denial means, how to rid ourselves of our material and sensual attachments, and what peace and inner joy this brings.

I became a hermit for six weeks. In a way I "left the world" and abandoned most creature comforts. What tremendous insights and fulfillments I received!

I met a semanticist who became a hermit in the Greek mountains for six months. He claimed it took that long to rid himself of the shackles of our materialistic world, to set himself really free. In addition, he fasted. He declared that his thinking became much clearer and that he experienced great insights into reality and visions of truth.

Now I firmly believe in moderation in all things. And I think that much of what is wrong today in the world, in society, is the lack of moderation on the part of people.

We've tried everything else, every other way, so let's give moderation a try.

Reflection Questions

What happens when there is excess in my life?
When am I happiest in life?

Suffering Is in Everyone's Life

Whatever is alive grows at least for a while. As persons, we want to grow continuously, to gain new awarenesses, to see new horizons. But growth involves change, transformation, pain—suffering.

Experience constantly confirms that we cannot produce what is truly worthwhile unless we pay the cost in effort, in suffering. This is one of the lessons and mysteries of life. This is the way we learn, mature, accomplish, and at last attain our full growth, when we suffer because of love and with love.

Think of the truly great artists. How many can you name who reached their best achievements without years of work, self-denial, discipline, tension, insecurity, heartache, disappointment, loneliness, and other forms of suffering? Among artists we include leaders, philosophers, writers, saints, and others too. A person who has not known suffering is unlikely to have learned anything important to tell us about life.

This is the reason why so many societies reverence their elders. Having experienced long life, they have endured suffering and thereby they know. New life and awareness have resulted. They have reached that treasured higher level of wisdom.

In our society, too, the elders have much to share with us. They have listened, observed, absorbed, endured. We must now listen to them and maintain a constant dialogue with them. Thus we supplement our own experience and enrich our lives with their accumulated treasures of wisdom, their store of insights, their awareness.

Observing the antics of some young people, George Bernard Shaw once cried: "What a precious gift youth is! What a shame it must be wasted on the young!" Would that some of that energy and vitality could be given to our elders who would know how to put it to good use while sharing their wisdom with others. This is another of those mysterious truths of life.

Reflection Questions

What have I learned through my suffering?

Have I grown in wisdom through the years?

Theme: *Active and Alive*

Essays: *Involve Me*

Liberation

I Have Power

Involve Me

"Tell me, I'll forget. Show me, I may remember. Involve me, I'll understand," says an old Chinese proverb.

As a teacher, I know that I am really learning a subject when I teach it to someone. I may have taken the same course and received an A, but not until I once teach that course do I really begin to know it, to understand it.

People in social work tell you that to be effective in that profession you can't be just a spectator or observer: you have to make the plunge and get involved. You don't just visit a soup kitchen and look on; you get in there and help serve, help clean up, have soup with the guests.

We hear a lot of Monday morning quarterbacking, usually by people who were not involved in the decision making process, who were not part of the action or execution of the plan, who certainly do not know all the facts. Usually they are harshly critical. And usually those being criticized are being "damned if you do and damned if you don't."

It is easy to sit back and criticize when we are not involved. "The caravan keeps moving while the dogs bark." It seems that in life there will always be dogs barking. Thank God, some caravans keep moving.

"If you are not a part of the solution, then you are part of the problem." Some people look at life and see only problems. Living is equated to problem solving. We really can't be utterly passive in life, merely spectators. We have to be part of the action. You have to declare your side and work for it.

"Not to make a decision means that you have already decided." There's no "non-committal" section in life. If you believe that you are there, then you are already committed to something, the status quo, non-involvement, "don't care," isolation, procrastination, etc.

I think we all feel the way the Bible says, "I wish you were hot or cold, not lukewarm." We want people who are with us entirely, not halfheartedly.

There comes a time in life when we have to stand up and be counted, when we have to show our true colors. Do it. That time is now.

Reflection Questions

Have I gotten involved when I felt I should?
What wrong have I righted lately?

Liberation

Why do we oppress each other? That is the evil of racism, sexism, ageism and so many other "isms."

We oppress children. In a parking lot I heard some man berating someone in a vulgar manner. I was surprised to see a little girl wilting in front of him. He even threatened her with violence.

I know a young man who feels called to work with young children, but his family insists that he be a "hard hat" construction worker. We oppress young people.

Some social workers and nurses are victims of "burnout," emotionally and physically exhausted. Studies show that the "system" under which they work may be the oppressor. The system could be any kind of organization, political or economic, a corporation, a church, a government or a bureaucracy which oppresses people.

George Burns, as God in "Oh God," remarks, "Don't blame it on me; you've done it." Yes, we've messed up the environment, we've caused wars, our mechanisms fail and cause accidents. God certainly doesn't. He gives life and wants life. We seem to hurt and destroy.

In a psychological study, members of a class were divided into prisoners and jailers. After some hours, the project was called off because the jailers became too oppressive—even violent—toward the prisoners, their classmates.

Something bad happens when we exert power over another human being. We become less of a human being. Power corrupts; absolute power corrupts absolutely.

A friend is someone who leaves you with all your freedom intact. We have to let others be. Give them space and allow them to grow.

God has given us free will. Many of us abuse it. We have plane crashes, we've polluted the atmosphere, we engage in war and hatred, but it's we who are doing it, not God.

We—one and all—are unique, beautiful, special. God has a plan for each one of us. Give children love and freedom to grow and be. Don't oppress them or fit them into your pattern. The foundation for their discipline must be love, as also in teaching children self-control and moderation.

Allow everyone, young, old, middle-aged, to be. God gives us all life and keeps us in existence. Why do we oppress and categorize people and lock them into boxes?

Maybe without oppression and with freedom to be, we would see a new world around us, a healthy, happy world at peace.

Reflection Questions

Do I know what my gifts are and what others' gifts are?

Do I give freedom to others or do I want control?

I Have Power

Every one of us has power to make changes in the world. What we think, how we feel, does influence the decision makers in our society.

Marketing—for example—means the selling of our products. Merchants want to know what you want or need, what pleases you, what hooks you into buying their wares. Billions of dollars are spent in marketing, to find out what you want.

Then there's television. We are the ones who really determine what we see on TV. Again, researchers find out what we want, what interests us, what we watch, and that determines the programming.

Politicians are continually consulting polls to find out what we are thinking about, what pleases us, what are the issues, and how we feel about them.

Public opinion stopped the war in Vietnam—another example of your power to change policies, to influence decision making.

I attend many executive meetings dealing with different groups of people. Our main concern always is: "What does the group want?" We can't even bring up a subject which we know the entire group is against because we would merely be wasting time.

All our bosses, leaders, officials, are concerned with what we want. So let them know what you want. Let your opinion be heard. You have power.

You have often heard it said: "You can't fight City Hall." Let me tell you, you can topple City Hall—or a Capitol building, for that matter—by the dynamic power of public opinion. Let them know what you think; organize others into groups; unite. Here in America we have the power to do anything we want, to change any repression or injustice.

Still more: we definitely do have the power to change the world, to make our world what it should be, to right every wrong.

Reflection Questions

When have I seen public opinion change something?

Am I part of an organization that brings about change for good?

Do It!

Recently I was on a committee evaluating the needs of the Tenderloin, a depressed area in downtown San Francisco. One of the hard questions we asked was, "What agencies are trying to bring about social changes for the betterment of the people in the Tenderloin?"

The surprise was that although many services exist to *alleviate* distress, only one or two were trying to change the conditions that *cause* it.

Most existing agencies have as their purpose the protection of visitors in the Tenderloin and taking care of certain needs of the elderly, the unemployed, the alcoholic, the poor, the disabled, the mentally ill, the sick, the victims, the hungry, the destitute, the battered. But so very few get to the causes of all these problems.

In social help, three levels of service exist:

(1) Direct Aid—food, clothing, housing, medication;

(2) Rehabilitation—education, job training, procuring employment;

(3) Reconstruction—changing the structures that cause poverty, advocacy, correcting certain laws and procedures, humanizing our society.

We need a balance of all three levels of service. Certainly we can't tell the starving person to wait until we get to the roots of poverty and so change the system that brings it about. So we try to relieve the crisis (as by feeding the hungry) and in addition to bring about social change so that poverty and hunger will no longer exist.

We strive to encourage the person to be in charge of his or her own life. We try to bring life, love, hope and help to the needy, that they may grow, may be liberated and free, may be a part in any decision that affects them. We support their efforts to become independent rather than being content to be dependent and kept down. We strive to be advocates for the disenfranchised, the powerless, the neglected.

Just giving direct aid can be counter-productive. That can widen the gap between the "have's" and the "have not's." It can keep encouraging people to remain dependent. So there has to be both rehabilitation and also social change in addition to direct aid.

Ask yourself: "What agencies are bringing about social change and betterment in my community? What agencies are helping the elderly to help themselves and others, trying to give them independence, space to grow, responsibility for their own lives, promoting participation in decisions by those affected?"

I think you will find the answers, and you'll find something that you can do. DO IT!

Reflection Questions

What have I done lately to better the situation of my neighbor? Do I talk a good game but never get in and play it?

Is There Hope?

Where is this all going to end? Half the world seems to be security guards, the other half robbers.

It's become a truism to complain about lack of safety. You dare not walk at night. You may be mugged in daytime. Bar your doors and windows! Double-lock everything! We're becoming an armed state. Our people feel the need to isolate themselves behind a barricade of locks, safeguards, security systems, barriers of many kinds. Will this ever stop?

Public equipment has to be built to take violent abuse, to hold up against vandalism. We have to put security police on vehicles of public transportation to deter thievery, destruction of property, mistreatment of passengers. Some have gone into a subway car and set fire to seats for no apparent reason. Walls are paint-sprayed, seats are ripped out. Whatever can be stolen is stolen, whatever can be destroyed is destroyed. Everything has to be secured, protected.

Are you fully aware of the violence and lack of discipline in some of our schools? Have you heard of the outrages committed by some students on others, including teachers? Have you evaluated the products of our educational system? Can the students talk clearly? Can they write intelligently and logically? Can they read and understand? Can they listen and express themselves? I teach on the graduate level and am appalled at the lack of training and talent evident even there.

I have never been able to understand wanton vandalism. Were we not taught to respect property rights and to be honest? To value and protect nature's beauty and treasures? To revere life?

A while back I visited the zoo, where we were taken on the tour in a jitney. Although there were parents and some guards in sight, there was no order. Some young people had jumped on without paying. Noisily they disrupted the entire educational and pleasure value of the visit. I thought to myself, "What is in store for them, and others not so young? What will their future be?"

I feel that the answer is that we need strong families. We need good mothers and fathers who instill moral principles in their children. Without such guidance there seems to be no hope. Parents have to be moral, healthy, normal and happy, living examples, exercising control. Then the children will pick this up and follow through. We have to activate strong family life.

And we have to provide strong religious and moral training through our ministers, priests and rabbis, our churches and synagogues. We need the firm structures of family and religion to help restore some moral fiber and muscle to our society, our communities.

Our schools should be the continuation of education begun by our parents and continued by them from the first moment of the child's life. Schools should be under the supervision of the parents because they are an extension of the parents' right to educate their children. Parents have to make sure that they know what their children are being taught. Schooling should supplement—not substitute for—education by the parents.

I ask, "Where is this all going to end?" The answer depends

on parents, families, and religion. Can we reverse the current ugly trend? I, for one, believe that we can. There is hope.

Reflection Questions

Is there violence and vandalism in my neighborhood? What do I do about it?

Do I use my influence as a citizen to better the educational system?

Who Does My Thinking?

Should one mistake, one minute, ruin an entire lifetime? At times it does. Why? When evaluating a person, should we not look at the entire lifetime, the thrust, the accomplishments, the character, the "track record"? How can we in justice take one infinitesimal part of someone's life span and pronounce judgment on all his or her years according to that moment?

I know that sounds illogical, but that is the way we act. One instant, one incident, one mistake, and we condemn.

I have a friend who made a mistake, used poor judgment, was arrested. Never before had he committed such an offense, but because of that one imprudent moment the rest of his life was jeopardized.

Then, only recently, I read in the papers of an outstanding achiever in the law profession, a charitable man developing legal aid services for the poor and for minorities. So highly regarded were his abilities that he was chosen to be dean of a famous law school. Late one evening, after a long and tiring work day, he made a mistake and was arrested. Subsequently he lost his job as dean. His career in law was ended. How pitiable! What a waste! Why do we do this to people?

If a person rings a bell once in his lifetime, we don't call him a bell-ringer. If someone prepares one meal in her lifetime, we don't call her a chef. Should we call someone a robber, cheat, murderer or immoral in some way, just because of one act or accusation? I admit it is sometimes possible that one act can betray one's impulses, and can sum up, reflect and reveal the misdeeds of a lifetime, but that is not what I am talking about. I refer to acts that do not belong to the pattern of the person's character.

I know that in professions such as teaching and the ministry, one act of imprudent behavior or even an impulsive remark can end a productive and noble career, a lifetime of good work. This outrages my sense of justice. We should weigh what people do in perspective of what they have done over the years, what their life and accomplishments have been, in addition to their physical, mental and emotional condition at the time of the reported misstep. Good and bad traits are in each of us. Hopefully the good dominates, the good intention, the thrust, the values and the ideals.

As a Christian I have been taught to forgive. In many cases people learn from their mistakes and become better persons, stronger and perhaps more compassionate. I believe in forgiving others, in giving others a second chance, especially when there is a well-founded hope for the future. Sometimes trust in another person can bring out the best in him or her.

A friend of mine committed a serious violation of the law. He came to me for help in the form of a reference for him. I was able to provide what he wanted, and I saw to it that additional aid was given to him. He looked at me in surprised disbelief and inquired, "Aren't you afraid of ruining your reputation and the good name of your institution by befriending and associating with me?" I smiled and assured him that this was a clear case of acting on my beliefs. I truly believed in him, in charity, forgiveness, and trust, and this was exactly what I was doing. That man is now at peace with the law and with society, happily married and in an excellent job, respected by all who know him.

Think about it.

Reflection Questions

Do I think for myself or do I accept everything without questioning or evaluating?

Have I taken risks for what I believe in?

Theme: Looking Back and Forth
Essays: Nostalgia—Good or Bad?
Ageism—A Hidden Prejudice
Let's Start Over

Nostalgia—Good or Bad?

Recently my philosopher friend told me that nostalgia starts early in life. High school students dream about grammar school days; those in their twenties mentally relive their youthful escapades. Popular art is full of nostalgia. Notice the popularity of antiques and the reflections of past decades in our clothing.

Nostalgia is a part of life. Formerly referring mainly to homesickness, it is now that wistful yearning to re-experience any bygone time or condition. We all retain memories that we mull over and replay in the theater of the mind and heart. Sometimes it takes just a trifling sensation, an odor, sound, picture or passing event to trigger the nostalgic process. Some people spend many moments in nostalgia—too many, perhaps.

"What were you doing when you found out about President Kennedy's death?" Some memorable dates are often relived in nostalgia.

Today a popular form of journalism is autobiography, the

narrative of your own life journey, your own story. Each one is unique and beautiful.

Christmas trees, presents, the appetizing fragrance of the turkey feast, carols, Auld Lang Syne, hard candy, relatives, bowl games—the holidays are wrapped in nostalgia. Then we want to be with those we love. We phone, we travel, we celebrate together. We recall previous holidays. We follow family traditions and recall family history. In religion, we go through festive rituals.

Like everything else, nostalgia is good—in the right proportion. It can be pleasant and joy-filling. And future planning is good too, important, needed. The past helps us to understand, determine and prepare for the future. We certainly cannot neglect the present. Let us not look back in anger nor forward in fear but around in awareness.

I enjoy my nostalgic moments. I treasure my family, my roots, my history, my growing up, my friends, the peaks and valleys of my life. And so, I am sure, do you with your own. Nostalgia is sweet at any age—and the final consolation of those who have lost all but memories.

Reflection Questions

Do I look back in anger or forward with fear? Why?

Do I enjoy my past and also my dreams for the future?

Ageism—A Hidden Prejudice

As human beings we label or pigeon-hole people. We try to find an easy index to a complex reality. This, of course, leads to rash and superficial judgments. Oftentimes we form fixed opinions on a person just because of externals: clothing, skin color, body shape, hair length, age, accent.

Many organizations are stubbornly prone to classify people strictly by age. Yet the number of one's years does not determine the capabilities of the person. Why is a person told to retire at sixty-five? Chronologically the count may be correct, but mentally the person may be healthfully mature and at the full height of intellectual acumen. Many an older person is full of energy, potentiality, and creativity, while emotionally more stable than ever before. Rich experience inspires such a person to new ideas. To retire a person so valuable is an injustice to a human being and a loss to society.

We have known people who retired mentally and physically at forty or even thirty-five, yet still went through the motions of holding a job. On the other hand, we know some in their seventies and eighties who are mentally alert and productive. Rather than base a person's qualifications for a job on chronological age, I think we should base it on productivity, whether the worker is twenty, or forty, or sixty, or ninety. If we ask a person to retire, let it be not because of age, but because of being unable to perform necessary duties of the job.

Some will protest that statistics say otherwise. My answer to them is that statistics deal with averages. I deal with individuals.

It's time to put "ageism" right along with the other prejudices—racism and sexism. Employers should not be permitted to discriminate merely by age.

We should group together in societies and other organizations as in friendships, not according to age but by reason of interests. This makes for richness and variety in life. Age does not mean that much to me. When I converse with someone, it's an exchange of ideas and feelings. People of various ages and I have been in tune, understand each other, and appreciate each other. Age has not clouded the issue.

I knew of a lady whose birth certificate was destroyed in the 1906 San Francisco fire. She decided to take ten years off her age, and presented herself as ten years younger. She worked for the city until the compulsory retirement age of sixty-five (in reality she was seventy-five) and then enjoyed many years of "retirement." She did not let age bog her down. More power to her—and to you who think young!

Reflection Questions

Does my age make a difference in my life? In what ways?
Do I use my age as an excuse? Do I like my age?

Let's Start Over

The older I get the less I can understand man's inhumanity to man. I see more and more of it, but I understand less and less. I see vindictive people hurting one another, punishing each other, and, in spite of all preaching, not loving or helping one another. I see it happening in families, among "loved ones," in businesses, in communities, among nations.

In spite of learned explanations—social, psychological, biological—there are other things too that I can't comprehend, such as vandalism and rape (sex should always be in a setting of love). I just can't understand why a person does these things or how his or her mind works.

A friend is someone who leaves you with all your freedom intact. Let the other be! Power over another human being destroys the one who has the power. Possessing another human being hurts both of those involved.

How frequently we hear people criticizing each other, backbiting, "You're damned if you do and damned if you don't." Many are jealous of one another, put down one another physically and psychologically, finding all sorts of ways to hurt one another. Some are dishonest; some steal from the other. Everywhere we see people use and abuse others.

The answer to all this is that we really have to make a fresh start in our attitudes. Let's get rid of those tendencies toward envy, flaw-picking, hate and jealousy. Let's begin to replace them with efforts to love one another, to be supportive of each other, to affirm the other.

We are all sinners; we are all messed-up; we are all weak, incomplete. But we do have the power to heal each other. If I express my "messed-up-ness" to my brothers and sisters, and yet they affirm me, accept me, love me, I am on the way to being whole, healed. This sounds too good to be true, but it is. Those who have tried this know. This is the fundamental therapy that operates in all good, healthy relationships.

Someone once suggested that at a certain time we all stop whatever we're doing, join hands, and tap-dance at the same time, all over the nation, all over the world. A crazy idea? It certainly is not as crazy as the arms race or atomic warfare. In fact, by comparison, I think it's a great idea.

When the unconventional artist Christo put his fence around the pastoral scenes of Sonoma County, California, many people exclaimed "He's crazy!" and "What a waste of money!" Yet maybe second thoughts are in order. I think "crazy" is the word for wars, hatreds, oppression, violence and all other methods of hurting people. I found the fence beautiful, uplifting—and human.

Let's start over! Let's treat all our brothers and sisters humanly.

Reflection Questions

What do I see as negative in my life? What is positive in my life? Do I judge life with the values of love and freedom?

Theme: Up, Up and Away

Essays: Smile!

From Dark to Light

Peace to You!

Smile!

A smile really puts me at ease. Barriers come tumbling down. My defenses relax. I am not threatened. I can talk; I can listen; I can be myself.

I think a lot of people are losing their sense of humor these days. They look so intense, as if they're carrying the whole world on their shoulders. Their faces are so unhappy, their expressions so dour.

Prophets of doom are all around us. "Things are all bad and getting worse," they shout.

Then we have the new messiahs who are going to save the world. They have all the answers. Usually their solutions are as simplistic as their rhetoric.

Human nature is rather constant; it remains the same. We have our good and bad qualities. They can change from generation to generation, but I assure you there will always be a mixture of good and bad—never all good or all bad.

Don't take yourself so seriously. Learn to laugh at yourself.

See your own shortcomings and the humor in others and all around you.

The other day I was happy to hear that even in the most solemn church ceremonies, if someone makes a funny mistake, the ministers feel free to respond as human beings. After all, this is what makes us different from the animal world—our risibility, our ability to laugh.

The best of men and women were able to laugh at themselves and not take themselves so seriously. They didn't think they were God's gift to mankind, though perhaps they were. Keep your sense of humor, develop it, use it, enjoy it.

Don't be uptight and get caught up in the rat race. Make sure you have enough time each day to relax, to rest, to recreate, to re-create yourself. Make leisure time for yourself to do the things you enjoy, to create, to think and evaluate. If you don't do this, you will begin getting on others' nerves and your own, and you won't grow as a person.

Once a rather rotund Jewish gentleman was supposed to meet Pope John XXIII. He felt reticent about it, he a Jew meeting the head of Catholicism. But friends assured him: "Pope John is a good, approachable human being." He went in with the others to meet the pope. He tried to stay in the background. Pope John came out, smiled as always, looked at everyone, and then went up to the Jewish gentleman, embraced him, and exclaimed, "Thank God there is someone as big as I am here today. Now I don't have to feel too self-conscious."

Keep your sense of humor. It'll keep you up.

Reflection Questions

Do I ever laugh at myself or do I usually take myself seriously? Do I like a sense of humor in others?

From Dark to Light

"If I accept the sunshine and warmth, I must also accept the thunder and lightning," says Kahlil Gibran. We love the summer and we try to escape the winter. We hate hardship and suffering. We love bliss and ecstasy. Yet life involves both extremes.

Experience demonstrates to each of us that hardships, suffering, setbacks, disappointments, failures, sins, sorrows and depression are part of everybody's life, yours and mine. We may fantasize life as being otherwise, but that is not reality.

There's a saying among bodybuilders, "No gain without pain." Exercise, workouts, diets and practice take time and require discipline, sacrifice and suffering. But by them we pay for the privilege of acquiring a stronger and better body. So it is also in other spheres of life.

Artists tell us of the labor, drudgery, perseverance and soul-searching efforts they have to put into their projects. "One percent inspiration, ninety-nine percent perspiration." Experience confirms: nothing of real value is accomplished without work and effort.

Muscles unused, untensed, unexercised, atrophy. Likewise life without hardship is weak and flabby. Yet an ever increasing part of our population wants, expects, even demands, all sorts of benefits without doing anything necessary to earn them by work or by sacrifice of their leisure. In their lives they expect nothing but sunshine and warmth—with no thunder or lightning.

Nature continues to teach us this lesson. After the chill in the dead of winter comes the season of spring with new life and bloom and warmth. The bright dawn follows the dark night.

The seemingly dead seed goes into the soil and comes up with life and greenery.

Out of hardship and suffering emerge stronger and better people. They have weathered the storms. Now they are more compassionate, sensitive, perceptive of others. If we calmly and patiently endure setbacks, sorrows and sufferings, we can become better and more understanding through them. One who has neither endured a struggle nor survived adversity is unlikely to have much wisdom or life to share with others. You can't understand the day unless you have been through the night.

I was talking with an old black gentleman who had led a hard life. Work and struggle were his everyday lot. He had to put up with poverty and prejudice. He had been oppressed, treated with contempt, "put down" repeatedly. Yet this man was at peace with himself and with others; he had only good things to say. I sensed a strong inner peace and security in him. He shared with me his vision of life and living. Actually he did not talk much. It was his demeanor and manner that revealed his charity, love and peace. He had an inner happiness and strength that could not be taken away from him. He had accepted the thunder and lightning of his life, and now he was enjoying and understanding life's sunshine and warmth.

Reflection Questions

Do I see the positive possibilities in the problems of my life?

Do I break through the darkness of my life to find the light?

Peace to You!

Like everything else, peace begins with us. I have to be at peace with myself before I can bring peace to others, to my family, my community, my city, my country, my world. Peaceful people are those who know and accept themselves, their strong points and weak ones. They like themselves.

An untroubled person has happy thoughts and knows inward comfort, spends more time thinking of others, is creative, ever positive, never negative. There is always so much to be done, so many new ideas to be clarified, so much to be shared.

In a city of noise and violence, in a life that is a struggle for sweet survival, we all yearn for a measure of peace. We want to tell the world around us to stop so we can withdraw into ourselves and find some inner calm and quiet. After all, that is where it must begin.

Actually, what is around us makes little difference when we gain the knack of cutting outside contact for a while, maintaining the center of complete tranquility within. We can do this in a crowded bus, in a noisy apartment house, or in the silent privacy of our room or of nature around us. We find this rest, this harmony, this center within. Then we can meditate.

Peacemakers are mediators and ombudspersons. They establish communication, effect reasonable compromise, produce harmony. They shun harsh criticism. They are not prophets of doom. They are never abusive of others, never expose others to ridicule, never indulge in violent opposition. They respect the freedom of everyone, even of those who abuse their freedom. They do not pronounce judgment on others. They do not misuse power even for a good end. They are at peace with themselves and therefore can share this peace with others, can bring it to others. To the center of peace within, they bear witness.

Perhaps you know the Hebrew word for goodness, harmony, peace—shalom!

Reflection Questions

Where do I find peace within myself, my life?

Do I bring peace to others?